MOVIE THEMES

FOR CLASSICAL PLAYERS

To access recorded piano accompaniments online, visit:
www.halleonard.com/mylibrary

"Enter Code"
2860-3518-5617-7740

ISBN: 978-1-5400-3706-0

HAL•LEONARD®

Visit Hal Leonard Online at
www.halleonard.com

Contact Us:
Hal Leonard
7777 West Bluemound Road
Milwaukee, WI 53213
Email: info@halleonard.com

In Europe contact:
Hal Leonard Europe Limited
42 Wigmore Street
Marylebone, London, W1U 2RN
Email: info@halleonardeurope.com

In Australia contact:
Hal Leonard Australia Pty. Ltd.
4 Lentara Court
Cheltenham, Victoria, 3192 Australia
Email: info@halleonard.com.au

HOW TO USE HAL LEONARD ONLINE AUDIO

Because of the changing use of media, and the fact that fewer people are using CDs, we have made a shift to companion audio accessible online. In many cases, rather than a book with CD, we now have a book with an access code for online audio, including performances, accompaniments or diction lessons. Each copy of each book has a unique access code. We call this Hal Leonard created system "My Library." It's simple to use.

Go to www.halleonard.com/mylibrary and enter the unique access code found on page one of a relevant book/audio package.

The audio tracks can be streamed or downloaded. If you download the tracks on your computer, you can add the files to a CD or to your digital music library, and use them anywhere without being online. See below for comments about Apple and Android mobile devices.

There are some great benefits to the My Library system. *Playback+* is exclusive to Hal Leonard, and when connected to the Internet with this multi-functional audio player you can:

• Change tempo without changing pitch
• Transpose to any key

Optionally, you can create a My Library account, and store all the companion audio you have purchased there. Access your account online at any time, from any device, by logging into your account at www.halleonard.com/mylibrary. Technical help may be found at www.halleonard.com/mylibrary/help/

Apple/iOS

Question: On my iPad and iPhone, the Download links just open another browser tab and play the track. How come this doesn't really download?

Answer: The Safari iOS browser will not allow you to download audio files directly in iTunes or other apps. There are several ways to work around this:

• You can download normally on your desktop computer, saving the files to iTunes. Then, you can sync your iOS device directly to your computer, or sync your iTunes content using an iCloud account.
• There are many third-party apps which allow you to download files from websites into the app's own file manager for easy retrieval and playback.

Android

Files are always downloaded to the same location, which is a folder usually called "Downloads" (this may vary slightly depending on what browser is used (Chrome, Firefox, etc)). Chrome uses a system app called "Downloads" where files can be accessed at any time. Firefox and some other browsers store downloaded files within a "Downloads" folder in the browser itself.

Recently-downloaded files can be accessed from the Notification bar; swiping down will show the downloaded files as a new "card", which you tap on to open. Opening a file depends on what apps are installed on the Android device. Audio files are opened in the device's default audio app. If a file type does not have a default app assigned to it, the Android system alerts the user.

CONTENTS

Pianists on the recordings: [1]Brendan Fox, [2]Ruben Piirainen

The price of this publication includes access to companion recorded piano accompaniments online,

for download or streaming, using the unique code found on the title page.

Visit **www.halleonard.com/mylibrary** and enter the access code.

Waltz for Peppy

from the Motion Picture *The Artist*

Composed by Ludovic Bource

Slowly, with freedom

Themes from *Cinema Paradiso*

By Ennio Morricone
and Andrea Morricone

CINEMA PARADISO
Simply, with feeling

LOVE THEME (TEMA D'AMORE)

*A cut may be made to measure 37.

Faster, with movement

Rubato (slower)

This page has been intentionally left blank to facilitate page turns.

Theme from E.T.
(The Extra-Terrestrial)
from the Universal Picture *E.T. (The Extra-Terrestrial)*

Music by John Williams

The Godfather
(Love Theme)
from the Paramount Picture *The Godfather*

By Nino Rota

Slowly and expressively

Theme from "Jurassic Park"

from the Universal Motion Picture *Jurassic Park*

Composed by John Williams

Mia & Sebastian's Theme

from *La La Land*

Music by Justin Hurwitz

As fast as possible, freely

Fast

Theme from "Lawrence of Arabia"

from *Lawrence of Arabia*

By Maurice Jarre

Gabriel's Oboe
from the Motion Picture *The Mission*

Music by Ennio Morricone

The Pink Panther

from *The Pink Panther*

By Henry Mancini

Swing (♪♪ = ⌐3¬♪♪)

8ba - - - - - - - - - - - - - - - ⌐

Tempo I (straight eighths)

He's a Pirate

from Pirates of the Caribbean: The Curse of the Black Pearl

Music by Hans Zimmer,
Klaus Badelt and Geoffrey Zanelli

Romeo and Juliet
(Love Theme)
from the Paramount Picture *Romeo and Juliet*

By Nino Rota

Slowly and expressively

Scene d'amour
from *Vertigo*

By Bernard Herrmann

Lento

Molto largamente e appasionato

Molto largamente e appasionato al fine